For my husband and my son~

The loves of my life, thank you for helping me become the woman I have always wanted to be. And loving all of me. Even the not so great parts.

She Hustles Cookbook by Jessie Staeger

Copyright @ 2019 by SheHustlesCookbook.com & Jessie Staeger Media All rights reserved.

Books may be purchased in quantity and/or special sales by contacting the publisher, Lulu Press Inc, or the author by email at jstaeger7@gmail.com

No part of this book may be reproduced in any written, electronic, recording, or photocopying without written permission of the publisher or author. The exception would be in the case of brief quotations embodied in critical articles or reviews and pages where permission is specifically granted by the publisher or author.

Although every precaution has been taken to verify the accuracy of the information contained herein, the author and publisher assume no responsibility for any errors or omissions. No liability is assumed for damages that may result from the use of information contained within.

All rights reserved for translation into foreign languages.
ISBN 978-1-79489-060-2
Printed in the United States of America

Contents

- **Introduction** — pg 5
- **Cocktails** — pg 6
- **Salads** — pg 9
- **Main Dishes** — pg 18
- **Give Me All The Sides!** — pg 39
- **Time To Wake Up Food!** — pg 47
- **Snack Time** — pg 50
- **Crockpot Goodies** — pg 54
- **The Good Shit! (desserts)** — pg 59
- **Salad Dressings, Sauces & Seasonings** — pg 65

Okay Jessie what the hell did you create here?

Well I create a Cookbook with my own twist.
Throughout this book you will find my smart ass comments, jokes, tips and some food that I have concocted, stole from other people and added my own twists to.
Erik and I attempt to be healthy when we're cooking at home. But let's be honest here, when we go out to eat. We eat like shit and drink! That's the fun part of going out right?!? Oh and don't worry I've added a few of my famous get drunk shots that I make for parties and good drinks.
I really hope you enjoy it. This it's not crazy long and I tried to be a straight to the point with the directions as I could be.

You'll find some really good recipes that look like you spent a shit ton of time in the kitchen, but you really did not. I'm all about work smarter not harder. Especially when it comes to food. I mean let's be honest who really wants to put in more work in the kitchen then you need to, right?!

Well kids grab yourself a drink and get cooking!

Ok! Let's start this cookbook off right! COCKTAILS! Cheers!

Sparkling Grapefruit Cocktails
1/4 c freshly squeezed grapefruit juice
1 1/2 oz citrus vodka
1 tbsp agave nectar
3-4 ice cubes
1/2 cup melon pomelo La Croix sparkling water
Directions
Combine grapefruit juice + vodka
add agave nectar and stir until dissolved
fill glass partway with ice
top with sparkling water

Blackberry Cucumber Skinny Mojito
2 blackberries
3 cucumber slices
3 sprigs of fresh mint
1.5-3 oz of Cruzan Key Lime Rum (or Cruzan Light Rum)
1 Blackberry Cucumber LaCroix
Ice
Directions
Add blackberries and mint to a highball glass and muddle them together using the back of a spoon. Place two cucumber slices into the glass, add ice, rum and top with LaCroix sparkling water. Garnish the rim of the glass with a slice of cucumber and serve.

Mind Eraser

In a rocks glass with ice, pour 1 ounce of Kahlúa and then float 2 ounces of vodka on top, pouring down the side of the glass so that it separates. Top with 2 ounces of club soda, poured down the side of the glass in the same way. Using two straws, suck the whole damn thing down.

Classic Margarita Done Right

To your blender add 4 cups of ice, 8 ounces tequila, 4 ounces fresh-squeezed lime juice, and 1.5 ounces of light agave. Blend it all up until good and frosty. Pour into glasses and garnish with lime wheels.

Irish Old Fashioned

In a mixing glass with ice, combine 2 ounces of Whiskey 12 Year and a ½ ounce of honey syrup (equal parts honey cut with hot water). Add 2 dashes each of orange bitters and Angostura. Strain into a rocks glass over ice. Garnish with a big twist each of orange and lemon peel, twisting both over the surface of the drink to spray their citrus oils all over.

Death in the Afternoon

Pour 1 ounce of absinthe and ½ of ounce cherry vodka into a Champagne flute and fill with sparkling wine (about 5 ounces). No garnish is necessary. You will thank me later:)

Big Papa

Equal parts Crown Royal and Root Beer or Cream Soda over ice.

Seriously good!

~Tonight I tried cooking with wine..... After 4 glasses I couldn't even remember why I was in the kitchen.

Fruity Vodka Party Punch

This is the perfect cocktail recipe for a party! This drink is full of lemonade and fruit punch, rum, and vodka and is the perfect easy punch recipe.

There's just something about a red fruit punch drink that makes me think tropical or fun…and it makes every party just that much better.

1 fifth vodka
1 2 liter of sprite
1 bottle of tonic water
2 cups Country Time Pink Lemonade mix

Add sliced lemons for garnish and enjoy, but be cautious she sneaks up on you:)

***** Want to kick up the party up a notch? With Shots? I DO!
Use half the amount of sprite and tonic water ADD 2 cups of clear rum to the mix!**

My Kinda Wine Spriters

1 bottle of red wine (a sweeter wine would be best)
4 cans of La Croix Mixed Berry Sparkling Water
3 shots of vodka
Ice, Frozen Blueberries, Strawberries or Raspberries.

This can be premade in a pitcher for guests ahead of time:)

*Random Tip~ Adding Sprite to shitty wine always makes it better!

SALADS

Chicken Fajita Salad

1 large red bell pepper, sliced thin lengthwise
1 large yellow bell pepper, sliced thin lengthwise
1 large orange bell pepper, sliced thin lengthwise
5 raw boneless, skinless chicken breasts, sliced thin lengthwise (about 7 oz. each)
1 large red onion, slice thin
1 tbsp garlic powder
1 tbsp onion powder
1 tbsp chili powder
1 tbsp ground cumin
1 tbsp olive oil

Directions
Saute' everything in a large pan, adding the spices about half way through.
Layer lettuce in the bowl, top with fajita chicken mixture, then top with clean salsa and/or Guacamole. Squeeze fresh lime over the top (optional)
   Taco Tuesday What!!!

~My cooking is fabulous... Even the smoke alarm cheers me on!

Strawberry Spinach Salad

Mix 2 generous handfuls fresh baby spinach,
1/3 cucumber diced,
Couple rings of red onion diced, a Handful of strawberries (tops removed & diced), almonds and drizzle with olive oil, fresh squeezed lemon juice, salt & pepper.

Perfect Summertime lunch or dinner!

Mediterranean Inspired Kidney Bean Salad

3 cans of kidney beans
1 red bell pepper - diced
1 yellow bell pepper - diced
1/2 red onion - diced
1 small bunch of parsley - chopped
2 lemons - juiced
1 tbsp olive oil
salt to taste
Directions
Start off with draining and rinsing the kidney beans, then toss them in a bowl or tupperware. Mix in your diced bell peppers, onion, and parsley. Drizzle the olive oil and mix well. Add desired amount of lemon. I love lemon so I will use two or more lemons. Salt to taste.
This recipe is extremely easy and very hard to mess up. You can always add and subtract ingredients, it's all up to your preference.

When I am making a big batch for a party I will add orange and green bell peppers to make it really colorful. It really doesn't matter what color bell peppers you use. I also add fresh minced garlic sometimes.

***Random Tip~How to tell if an egg is bad... Put it in a bowl of water if it floats. Throw that shit away :)**

Broccoli Apple Pear Cashew Salad

5 cups broccoli, cut into florets
1 apple, cored and diced
1 pear, cored and diced
1/4 cup red onion, finely chopped
1 cup cashews (toasted, optional)
1 cup dried cranberries
Dressing
1/2 cup mayonnaise
1/2 cup Greek yogurt
2 tbsp lemon juice
3 tbsp honey
Kosher salt and freshly ground pepper, to taste
Directions
In a medium bowl, whisk together mayonnaise and Greek yogurt, then stir in lemon juice and honey.
Season to taste with salt and pepper.
In a large bowl, combine broccoli florets, diced apple and pear, red onion, cashews and cranberries, and toss together to combine.
Pour dressing over broccoli mixture, then toss until everything is evenly coated.
Serve immediately or refrigerate for at least 20 minutes, giving flavors a chance to develop and build.

~Can we say party favorite! OH ya!

***Random Tip~Cottage cheese & sour cream will last twice as long if you turn the container upside down. This forms a vacuum & prevents bacteria.**

Coconut Roasted Carrot Salad

A ROASTED CARROT SALAD WITH COCONUT, ALMONDS, DRIED CHERRIES AND PLENTY OF MINT.

2 pounds carrots
1/4 cup sliced almonds
2 cloves garlic minced
2 tbsp coconut oil
1/2 cup feta cheese optional
1/4 cup dried cherries
1/4 unsweetened shredded coconut
2 tbsp extra virgin olive oil
1.5 tbsp apple cider vinegar
2 tbsp honey
handful of fresh mint thinly sliced

Directions

Preheat the oven to 400 degrees.
Wash, trim and peel carrots (if not using organic) and slice them diagonally into coins.
Add garlic, almonds, and carrots to a large bowl.
Melt coconut oil and pour over carrot mixture.
Add salt and pepper to taste and toss to combine.
Spread carrot mixture onto a baking sheet and bake for about 20 minutes, flipping/stirring a few times during roasting.

While carrots are roasting, whisk together the olive oil, honey and apple cider vinegar in a small bowl. Set aside.
Once carrots are finished roasting, remove from oven and let cool for about 10-15 minutes on the baking sheet.
Once cool, add carrot mixture to a large bowl with feta (if using) and dried cherries.

Pour the dressing into a bowl and toss to combine.
Garnish with the mint leaves before.
Looking for a good weekend meal or snack?

Cucumber Avocado Salad

2 tsp paprika
1/2 tsp thyme
1/2 tsp oregano
1/2 tsp dried onion
1/2 tsp garlic salt
1/2 tsp chili flakes pepper optional
2 dollops avocado oil
1 cup cooked chickpeas
1 cucumber
1 yellow bell pepper
1/4 cup chopped cilantro
1 avocado
1 tbsp olive oil
sea salt & pepper to taste
1 lime juiced

Directions

Preheat oven to 400F.
Add all spices to a bowl and whisk, then add avocado oil and mix well until creamy.
Add cooked chickpeas to spice mix and coat well. The coated chickpeas go into the preheated oven on a baking sheet for 20 minutes.
Wash and dice cucumber, bell pepper, cilantro. Deseed, peel and dice avocado and add all to a large mixing bowl.
Once chickpeas have cooled down you can add to salad and season with olive oil, sea salt, pepper and lime juice to taste

~Stupid healthy and filling. Perfect if your starving and watching you that sexy figure of yours :)

Chile Lime Salmon Fajita Salad w/ Cilantro Lime Vinaigrette

Salmon 1 pound skin on salmon
3 tbsp olive oil, divide
1 tsp chile powder
1 tsp smoked paprika
1/2 tsp cumin
zest of 2 limes
pinch of salt and pepper
1 red pepper, sliced

** Salads
8 cups spring greens mix, chopped
1 small jalapeno, seeded + chopped
1/3 cup cooked black beans, rinsed + drained if using canned
1-2 avocados, sliced fresh cilantro, for topping

**Simple Lime Vinaigrette
1/4 cup olive oil
1/4 cup fresh lime juice (about 2 limes)
2 tsp cilantro, chopped (or more to your liking)
1/2 tsp chili powder
salt and pepper, to taste

Directions

To make the dressing, combine the olive oil, lime juice, cilantro, chili powder, and salt and pepper. Whisk to combine, taste and adjust the seasonings to your liking. Set aside. In a large salad bowl add lettuce, jalapeño and black beans. Drizzle with the juice of half a lime (only do this if eating right away). Toss well and set aside.

In a small bowl combine the chili powder, smoked paprika, cumin, lime zest and a good pinch of salt and pepper.

**Place the salmon on a plate and rub with 1 tablespoon olive oil. Sprinkle the spice mixture over the salmon and gently rub it into the salmon. Heat a medium size skillet over medium-high heat. Add a tablespoon of olive oil and once hot, add red pepper slices and a pinch of salt and pepper. Stir fry the peppers for 4-5 minutes. Remove the peppers from the pan. Reduce the heat to medium and add another tablespoon of olive oil and add the salmon, skin side facing up. Sear the salmon for 3-4 minutes and then flip and continue cooking for another

4-5 minutes or until the salmon reaches your desired doneness. Cooking times will vary depending on the size of your salmon. Cut salmon into 4-6 pieces or chop into bites. To assemble the salads, add the red peppers to the salad bowl and toss. Divide the salad among plates or bowls. Top each bowl with a piece of salmon. Add a few slices of avocado and drizzle with dressing. Garnish with more cilantro.
ENJOY! THIS IS BOMB!

Chicken Taco Salad

2-3 Boneless Skinless Chicken Breasts, diced
4 Cups Chopped Romaine Lettuce
2 Medium Tomatoes, diced
1 Avocado, diced
1/2 Cup Black Beans Salsa
1/2 Red Onion, chopped
1/2 Red Pepper, diced
1 T Avocado or Olive Oil
1/2 Yellow Pepper, diced
Taco Seasoning
Avocado Dressing (Recipe Included)
Directions
Add olive oil, water and chicken to large skillet, evenly sprinkle with taco seasoning and cook over medium-high heat until cooked through. While chicken is cooking make the

**Avocado Dressing
In food processor add half an avocado, 1/4 cup plain yogurt
1 cup Cilantro Juice of a lime 1/2 tsp salt, and 1 clove of garlic. Blend until smooth.
Add Lettuce to bowl and evenly sprinkle with tomatoes, red onion, black beans, avocado, and chicken. Add desired amount of Avocado Dressing and Salsa.
Optional: Tortilla Chips.

Cucumber, Pear and Fennel Salad
Apple Cider Vinaigrette
1 apple, peeled, cored, and chopped coarsely
1/4 cup apple cider vinegar
1 tbsp lime juice
1 tbsp finely diced shallots
1 tsp brown sugar
1/4 cup olive oil
salt and pepper (to taste)
**Salad:
2 pounds of cucumber, diced into 3/4 inch cubes
1 fennel bulb, cut into 1/2 inch cubes
2 pears, cored and diced into 1/2 inch cubes
1/2 cup pomegranate seeds
Directions
**Vinaigrette:
To make the vinaigrette, puree apple, vinegar and lime juice in a blender until smooth. Strain mixture through a sieve, squeezing solids to get all the liquid from them. Add shallot and sugar, stirring until sugar dissolves. Add oil until well combined. Season with salt and pepper to taste.
Combine salad ingredients with ¾ cup of the vinaigrette.

Chickpea Salad Recipe
Two cans of chickpeas, rinsed and drained
½ cup roasted red and/or yellow peppers chopped
¼ cup sliced olives
⅓ cup sliced Cherry tomatoes
Small bunch of parsley, chopped Scallions, chopped Minced garlic Juice of one lemon Olive oil Salt and pepper Mix all ingredients and serve.

Quick & Easy Red Cabbage Salad

3 cups red cabbage, thinly sliced
2 cups romaine lettuce, thinly sliced
1/2 cup cherry tomatoes
1/2 cup sliced radishes, sliced
1/2 cup homemade vinaigrette dressing (I like avocado oil & coconut aminos)

Directions

In a large salad bowl, add red cabbage, romaine, cherry tomatoes and radish. Top the salad with dressing.

*Here is a little deliciousness that would make a great hearty meal!

Fennel and Pomegranate Quinoa Salad

1 cup dried quinoa
1 fennel bulb, cut into small cubes
2 tsp fennel fronds, coarsely chopped
2 stalks celery, cut into small cubes
1/4 cup mint leaves, torn into small pieces
seeds from 1 pomegranate
1 bunch radishes, cut into small cubes
1/2 cup chopped pecans
Apple Cider Vinaigrette
3 tsp olive oil
3 tsp apple cider vinegar
1 tsp packed brown sugar
1/2 tspDijon
salt and pepper

Directions

Cook quinoa according to package directions.
While quinoa is cooking, prep your salad ingredients.
Shake together the dressing.
Toss everything together and serve!

And for the….. I don't want a Damn Salad today! But I don't know what the hell I am Hungry for Sections :)

These are purposely all over the place to help figure out what your hinkiering for.
This is how my ADHD ass figures out what we are eating.
It's like Russian Roulette but for FOOD! Lol

Main Dishes

Chilli Glazed Salmon
3 servings
4 oz salmon, 3 fillets
½ cup chili sauce
¼ cup fresh scallions, chopped
Directions
Preheat oven to 400°F
In a bowl, mix together the salmon, chili sauce, and the scallions.
Place the fillets on a baking tray lined with parchment paper. Spoon any leftover sauce on top of the salmon.
Bake for 12-15 minutes, until the salmon is cooked but still tender.

Stupid Blackbeans and Rice
2 cups brown rice
1 balck beans
1 small jar salsa
1 small onion diced
Directions
Boil rice to box specs, drain then add a can of drained black beans with jar of salsa and dice onion cook over medium heat for 5 minutes and serve. This will keep up to a week in the fridge. Great side for any dish. (optional add fresh squeezed lime juice and cilantro at serving for a more refreshing dish)

Easy Beef & Cheese Enchiladas

1 pack of tortillas
1 ½ pound ground beef
1 small onion diced
3 cups shredded cheese (use fav cheese, we use the taco blend)
1 pack taco sauce
½ cup water
2 cans red enchiladas sauce
1 container of sour cream

Directions

Preheat oven to 350. Lightly spray a 9x13-inch pan with cooking spray.
In a large skillet, brown ground beef. Drain fat. Return meat to skillet. Stir in diced onion, taco seasoning with ½ cup of water mix well. Add 2 cups of shredded cheese. Cook over low heat until thoroughly heated.
Lightly pour a thin layer of sauce over bottom of 9x13-inch pan. Set rest of can to side.
Roll up tortilla and place seam side down in 9x13-inch pan. Repeat with remaining tortillas. (pack them tightly) Pour remaining sauce over tortillas. Top with remaining cheese.
Bake for 25-30 minutes, until cheese is melted and enchiladas are heated thoroughly with slight crisp to edges.
Take second can of sauce and heat. Add after enchiladas are plated. Top with sour cream
**Pairs great with refried beans and brown rice for a full meal.

*Random Tip~Running bacon under cold water before cooking will reduce shrinking by up to 50%! Sorry guys this only works for bacon :)

Baked Parmesan Garlic Potato Wedges

3-4 large potatoes, sliced into wedges
4 tbsp olive oil
2 tsp salt
2 tsp of garlic powder
2 tsp Italian seasoning
½ cup shredded Parmesan cheese
optional: fresh cilantro, ranch or blue cheese dressing for dipping
Directions
Preheat oven to 375. Lightly grease a large baking sheet and set aside. Place potato wedges in a large bowl. Drizzle with olive oil and toss to coat. In a small bowl whisk together salt, garlic powder, and Italian seasoning. Sprinkle potato wedges with shredded cheese, tossing to coat. Then place potato wedges on prepared baking sheet in a single layer with skin-sides-down. Bake for 25-35 minutes until potatoes are fork-tender and golden. Sprinkle with freshly chopped parsley and dressing for dipping.seasoning mixture.

Amazing Zucchini Pasta

3 large zucchini
4-5 tomatoes, seeded and diced
1 clove garlic, minced
1/2 cup raw olives, coarsely chopped
1/2 cup olive oil Himalayan salt and pepper to taste
20 fresh basil leaves
Directions
Peel zucchini or leave skin on. Spiralize zucchini into noodles or peel into fettuccini-like strips. Mix with a pinch of salt and let sit for 15-30 minutes. Combine tomatoes, garlic, olives, capers, olive oil, salt and pepper, reserving the basil. Let mixture rest at room temperature for 30 minutes to meld seasonings. Using a paper or kitchen towel, gently squeeze pasta to extract all the liquid. Place in large mixing bowl. Put half the pasta into the bowl along with 3/4 of the basil and gently toss. - I just threw it all in a bowl or divide into bowls. Top with the balance of pasta mixture and top with chopped tomatoes.

Popps Crab and Shrimp Seafood Bisque

3 tbsp butter
2 tbsp chopped green onion
2 tbsp chopped celery
3 tbsp all-purpose flour
2 1/2 cups milk
1/2 tsp freshly ground black pepper
1 tbsp tomato paste
1 cup heavy whipping cream
8 ounces crab meat
4 to 8 ounces small cooked shrimp or other seafood
2 tbsp sherry win

Directions

Melt the butter in a Dutch oven or large saucepan over medium-low heat; add the chopped green onion and celery. Saute, stirring, until tender.
Blend the flour into the butter and vegetables until well incorporated. Continue cooking, stirring, for about 2 minutes.
Warm milk in another saucepan over medium heat.
Slowly stir in the warmed milk and continue cooking and stirring until thickened.
Add freshly ground black pepper, tomato paste, and heavy cream.

Serve and Enjoy!

Super Fast Healthy Chicken and Rice

Boneless skinless chicken thighs marinated in EVOO and some apple cider vinegar, adobo spice, salt and pepper.
Oven roasted at 400F for 30 minutes.
Steamed brown rice with EVOO and salt and pepper

***Random Tip~EVOO= extra virgin olive oil**

Taco Spaghetti To Die For

1 tbsp olive oil
1 pound ground beef
1 (1.25-ounce) package taco seasoning
1 (10-ounce can) Ro*Tel® Mild Diced Tomatoes & Green Chilies
1 tbsp tomato paste
8 ounces spaghetti
1/2 cup shredded cheddar cheese
1/2 cup shredded mozzarella cheese
1 Roma tomatoes, diced
2 tbsp chopped fresh cilantro leaves.

Directions

Heat olive oil in a large stockpot or Dutch oven over medium high heat. Add ground beef and cook until beef has browned, about 3-5 minutes, making sure to crumble the beef as it cooks; stir in taco seasoning. Drain excess fat.

Stir in Ro*Tel, tomato paste, spaghetti and 3 cups water. Bring to a boil; cover, reduce heat and simmer until pasta is cooked through, about 13-16 minutes.

Remove from heat and top with cheeses. Cover until melted, about 2 minutes.

Serve immediately, garnished with tomato and cilantro, if desired.

*Random Tip~ Rub Canola/Olive Oil on your knives before cutting onions to prevent you from crying like a little biotch :)

Black Bean Quinoa Burgers

1 cup black beans
1 cup quinoa cooked
1 tsp cumin
Lime juice from 1/3 lime
Salt and pepper to taste
Cayenne pepper to taste
2 garlic cloves minced
1/3 yellow onion, finely diced
2 tbsp fresh cilantro, diced
1 tbsp coconut or olive oil

Directions

In a medium mixing bowl, mash the black beans with a fork. Mix with the quinoa and Then add the other ingredients. This will make 2-4 patties depending on how big you like them.

Heat the oil in a skillet over medium-high heat. When the oil is hot, fry the patties until they are nicely browned, about 5 minutes. Turn and fry the other side.

Sweet Hawaiian Crockpot Chicken Recipe

*Goes great with brown rice
1 cup pineapple juice
1/2 cup brown sugar, firmly packed
1/3 cup soy sauce, light
2 lb chicken breast tenderloins

Directions

Add all of the ingredients to the crockpot.
cook on low 6-8 hours and they should just fall apart.
Sweet Hawaiian Slow-Cooker Chicken only has 4 ingredients and cooks in your slow-cooker, so you can get a delicious dinner on the table with minimal effort.

Chicken & Rice Soup

3 Rotisserie Chicken, diced
½ large yellow onion, diced
2-3 stalks celery, diced
2-3 whole carrots, diced (or couple handfuls baby carrots, diced)
2 cups cooked brown rice OR quinoa
32 oz carton (low sodium) chicken broth
2-3 cups water
Sprig of fresh rosemary (optional)
Salt/Pepper to taste

Directions

Cook rice (or quinoa) according to package instructions.
Dice chicken & all veggies and place in 2+ quart pot with broth, water, rosemary, salt & pepper. Bring to boil, reduce heat to low medium, add rice and cook until veggies are tender (usually 1-1.5 hrs).
Or throw all ingredients in your crockpot on low all day (pre-cook rice so it doesn't suck up all your liquid.

Tortilla Soup

2 cans vegetable broth
2 cans stewed tomatoes
2 cans pinto beans, drained
2 cans black beans, drained
24 oz picante or salsa
1 sm-med onion, diced
2 tbsp homemade taco seasoning

Optional toppings: Rice chips, cheddar "cheese" shreds, avocado slices, green onions Drain/rinse beans. Add all ingredients to a large pot. Warm through & serve with chosen toppings.

Lime Chipotle Shrimp with Brown Rice and Asparagus

**Brown Rice – cook according to package directions
12 jumbo shrimp, peeled
Juice from1 lime
2 tbsp olive oil
½ tbsp ground red chipotle pepper
2 cloves garlic, minced
½ tsp sea salt
2 pounds of asparagus, tough ends trimmed, rinsed and patted dry
3 tbsp extra-virgin olive oil
1 1/2 tbsp minced garlic
Salt & ground black pepper
2 tsp fresh lemon juice
Shrimp
Directions
Combine all ingredients in a zip-lock baggie and marinate for at least 20 min. Heat skillet and add all ingredients, including the marinade, to the pan. Cook a few minutes on each side until the shrimp turns pink. OR, put marinated shrimp of a skewer and cook on a grill.
Brush marinade over shrimp as they cook. Cook a few minutes on each side until they turn pink. Serve over cooked brown rice.
**Asparagus Preheat the oven to 425 degrees F. In a large glass baking dish, toss the asparagus with the olive oil and garlic. Season lightly with Salt and pepper and toss. Bake until the asparagus are tender and lightly browned, 15 to 20 Minutes, depending upon the thickness of the stalks, stirring twice. Remove from the oven and toss with lemon juice. Adjust the seasoning, to taste

***Random Tip~ If you can't remember my name, just say……..
"SHOTS" and I'll turn around!**

Baked Salmon and Asparagus in Foil (stupid easy)

Skinless wild salmon fillets (no skin! Pro tip let salmon sit in cold water bath for 15 minutes to get rid of the strong fishy taste)
1 lb asparagus, tough ends trimmed
2 1/2 tbsp olive oil
2 cloves garlic, minced
Salt and freshly ground black pepper
1 lemon thinly sliced
Fresh chopped fresh thyme, rosemary or cilantro
Cooked brown rice or quinoa (cooked to package specs)

Directions

Preheat oven to 400 degrees. Cut four sheets of aluminum foil about 14-inch long. Divide asparagus into 4 equal portions (about 8 spears per foil packet) and layer in the center of each length of foil.

In a small bowl stir together oil with garlic. Drizzle 1 tsp of oil over portion of asparagus then sprinkle with salt and pepper. Rinse salmon and allow excess water to run off, then season bottom of each fillet with salt and pepper. Layer fillets over asparagus. Drizzle on top of each salmon fillet with 1 tsp of olive oil mixture and season top with salt and pepper to taste. Top each with about 2 sprigs of thyme, rosemary or cilantro and 2 lemon slices Wrap sides of foil inward over salmon then fold in top and bottom of foil to enclose.

Place foil pouches in a single layer on a baking sheet. Bake in preheated oven until salmon is cooked through, about 25 minutes. Unwrap and serve warm

*Random Tip~ Keep cake moist by eating it all in one sitting. Yea I know right! We have all been doing it wrong for years!

Chicken Zoodle Soup

Just like mom's cozy chicken noodle soup but made with zucchini noodles instead! So comforting AND healthy! 227.3 calories.

2 tbsp olive oil, divided
1 pound boneless, skinless chicken breasts, cut into 1-inch chunks
Kosher salt and freshly ground black pepper
3 cloves garlic, minced
1 onion, diced
3 carrots, peeled and diced
2 stalks celery, diced
1/2 teaspoon dried thyme
1/4 teaspoon dried rosemary
4 cups chicken stock
1 bay leaf
1 pound (3 medium-sized) zucchini, spiralized*
2 tbsp freshly squeezed lemon juice
1 sprig of rosemary
2 tbsp chopped fresh parsley leaves

Directions

Heat 1 tablespoon olive oil in a large stockpot or Dutch oven over medium heat. Season chicken with salt and pepper, to taste. Add chicken to the stockpot and cook until golden, about 2-3 minutes; set aside.

Add remaining 1 tablespoon oil to the stockpot. Add garlic, onion, carrots and celery. Cook, stirring occasionally, until tender, about 3-4 minutes. Stir in thyme and rosemary until fragrant, about 1 minute.

Whisk in chicken stock, bay leaf and 2 cups water; bring to a boil. Stir in zucchini noodles and chicken; reduce heat and simmer until zucchini is tender, about 3-5 minutes. Stir in lemon juice; season with salt and pepper, to taste.

Healthy Stuffed Peppers - And Still Freaking Good!

1 pound ground turkey
1 small onion
1 clove of fresh garlic, minced
2 (14.5 ounces) cans of organic diced tomatoes (drained)
1 (10 ounce) can of organic diced tomatoes with green chile peppers (drained)
1 (10 ounce) can of organic tomato sauce
7 ounces of brown rice
4 large green bell peppers

Directions

In a skillet over medium heat, cook ground beef and onion until evenly brown and onion is tender. Season with fresh garlic. Drain grease. Mix in all 3 cans of diced tomatoes. Reduce heat to low and simmer 15 minutes. Prepare rice according to package directions. Preheat oven to 375 degrees. Cut peppers in half and remove seeds. Arrange pepper halves in baking dish and fill each with rice and meat mixture. Pour can of tomato sauce over the filled peppers. If there is any remaining diced tomatoes and meat mixture pour it around peppers. Bake 55 minutes in preheated oven until bubbly.

Cod Fillets

Wild Caught Cod Fillets
2 tsp of olive oil or coconut oil for a tropical taste
Juice of one lemon
¼ tsp of salt & pepper
Dash of garlic salt to taste
Thin sliced roma tomatoes
Fresh bay leafs

Directions

Preheat oven to 425 degrees. Place fish in greased shallow baking dish. Combine oil and lemon juice; brush on fish. Sprinkle with salt, pepper and garlic salt. Place rotation of tomato and bay leaves on top of cod. Bake 4 to 6 minutes for each ½ inch of thickness or until fish flakes easily with a fork at the thickest part. Splash any leftover lemon juice as desired

Spicy Paprika & Lime Chicken

2 lbs. chicken tenderloins
5 tsps paprika
1 tsp cayenne pepper or chili powder
1 1/2 tsp Celtic salt or sea salt
1 tsp Allspice
1 tsp coriander seeds powder
1 tsp black pepper
3 tbsps olive oil
2 garlic cloves, finely chopped
2 tsps tomato paste
2 limes (zest + juice from one lime for the marinade and juice from the second when serving)
Olive oil for frying

Directions

Mix all marinade ingredients in a large bowl. Rinse chicken meat and cut larger pieces in half keeping long slices. Using your hands, cover and rub the pieces with the marinade. Cover with cling wrap and set aside for at least one hour before grilling. If using a grill plate or a frying pan on your stove, heat one teaspoon of coconut oil until sizzling hot. Fry chicken pieces for 3 minutes on each side and then remove to a plate to rest. Make sure not to overcrowd the frying pan or you will end up with too much meat juice and your dish will become stewed rather than grilled chicken. If using a BBQ, heat the plate to sizzling hot and either spray with olive oil or brush with coconut oil. Place chicken pieces on the plate with a little space in between and cook for 3 minutes on each side on medium/high heat with the lid on." Remove cooked chicken to a serving plate and drizzle with more lime juice before serving.

Preparation time: 10 minutes + at least 1 hour marinating time
Cooking time: 15 minutes depending on the size of frying pan/BBQ plate

Turkey, Kale and Brown Rice Soup

2 tbsp of olive oil
2 medium carrots, peeled and cut into ½ inch pieces
1 large red pepper, cut into ½ pieces
8 ounces ground white turkey meat, broken into small chunks
1 tsp of each of the following spices: oregano, thyme, salt, basil and two bay leafs
½ tsp of pepper
5 cups of (low sodium) chicken broth
1 (15 ounce) can diced tomatoes, drained
1 cup cooked brown rice
1 small bunch of kale, center ribs removed – leaves coarsely chopped

Directions

Heat olive oil in large pot over medium heat. Add carrots and red pepper and sauté until tender. Add turkey and stir until meat is white and just begins to brown. Add all spices. Add the broth diced tomatoes and cooked rice – bring to boil. Stir in kale. Reduce heat to medium/low, cover and simmer until vegetables are tender.

Almond Crusted Chicken

1 cup raw, unsalted almonds (or use almond flour/meal)
1-4 (as needed) Chicken Breasts (fresh or thawed)
Extra virgin olive oil
1 tsp sea salt
½ tsp black pepper

Directions

Preheat oven to 400 degrees. Grind raw almonds into flour/meal – use a food processor for about 1 minute. Place almond meal on a plate or bowl. Slice chicken breast into tenders. Baste or spray each tender with olive oil. Dip or roll each tender in almond meal.
Bake for 25 minutes or until golden brown on top

Tomato Basil Sandwiches

8 slices of favorite bread
2/3 cup Mozzarella Shreds
3 plum tomatoes, cut into thick slices
1 cup fresh basil pesto, recipe below (or use the store bought stuff OR Fresh Basil leaves)
Freshly ground black pepper
Extra-virgin olive oil
Directions
If you have a panini press, turn it on to warm up; otherwise, set a skillet over medium heat.
Assemble sandwich by smearing insides of bread slices with pesto. Arrange a layer of sliced tomato and season with a few turns of fresh pepper. Layer the mozzarella slices over the top and then place another piece of bread on top to make the sandwich.
Drizzle olive oil over skillet's surface and place sandwiches on the hot skillet or panini press. If using a skillet, place another heavy skillet over the top to form a "press". Turn after 2 to 3 minutes and replace weight. The sandwich is ready when golden brown and mozzarella has melted around the edges.

**Basil pesto

½ cup pine nuts
2 cups fresh basil leaves
1 cup fresh Italian parsley leaves
½ cup Parmesan
2 garlic cloves
¼ teaspoon salt
½ cup extra-virgin olive oil Toast pine nuts in a skillet over medium heat until fragrant, about 5 minutes. Combine pesto ingredients in a food processor and pulse until well combined but still rough-textured.

Garlic Margarita Chicken & Zucchini

1 lb. chicken breast, or tenders cut into 1" pieces
1 tsp olive, coconut or avocado oil
1 large garlic clove, crushed
1/4 tsp sea salt
Ground black pepper to taste
Zucchini & Tomatoes:
1.5 lbs. zucchini, cut into half-moon shapes
1.5 cups fresh, halved grape tomatoes
1 tsp olive, coconut or avocado oil
1 large garlic clove, crushed
1/2 tsp sea salt Ground black pepper, to taste
Garnish:1/4 cup fresh chopped Basil and a sprinkle parmesan/cheese shreds (optional)

Directions

For the Chicken: Preheat (cast iron) skillet on medium heat add oil to coat. Add garlic and cook for just 10 seconds. Then add chicken, sprinkle with sea salt and pepper to taste. Cook for 8-10 minutes uncovered, stirring occasionally. Transfer to a plate and set aside.

For the Zucchini and Tomatoes Cook the zucchini the same way as Chicken but for 6 minutes, adding tomatoes during the last 3 minutes of cooking time. Add chicken back to skillet and stir just to warm. Remove from heat, sprinkle with fresh Basil. Refrigerate in a glass airtight container for up to 5 days.

*Random Tip~Never wrap warm meat or poultry in aluminum foil and place it in the fridge. Foil is an insulator and the meat will stay warm longer. Which attracts bacteria and allows it to thrive!

Almond Crusted Chicken

1 cup raw, unsalted almonds (or use almond flour/meal)
1-4 (as needed) Chicken Breasts (fresh or thawed)
Extra virgin olive oil
1 tsp sea salt
½ tsp black pepper

Directions

Preheat oven to 400 degrees 2. Grind raw almonds into flour/meal – use a food processor for about 1 minute. Place almond meal on a plate or bowl. Slice chicken breast into tenders. Baste or spray each tender with olive oil. Dip or roll each tender in almond meal. Bake for 25 minutes or until golden brown on top

Spicy Braised Beef

2 lbs. lean beef eye round (or top round), trimmed of all fat
1 sweet onion, diced
1 red bell pepper, diced
2 garlic cloves, sliced
2 jalapenos
1/4 cup low sodium beef broth
1 cup canned diced tomatoes with juice
1 tbsp Coconut Aminos
2 tbsp fresh lime juice
1/2 tsp cumin
1/4 tsp oregano
1/4 tsp coriander

Directions

Add the beef to the slow cooker. Season with salt and pepper. Spread the onion, red pepper, garlic, and spicy peppers (whichever ones you choose) on and around the beef. Mix together the beef broth, tomatoes, coconut aminos, lime juice, cumin, oregano, and coriander. Pour over beef. Cook on low for 8 hours. Shred or slice. If you have time, leave the beef in the slow cooker on warm for 30 minutes after shredding to let more of the cooking liquid impart flavor in the beef.

Notes Use a green bell pepper for a version that isn't spicy.

Pepperoni Bread Recipe

1 Can pizza crust (or homemade)
6 oz of sliced Pepperoni
8 – 12 oz of 6 Cheese Italian Blend (or Mozzarella)
1/2 – 3/4 cup Parmesan cheese
Italian Dressing
Italian Seasoning
Garlic Powder
Egg White
Tomato or Pizza Sauce (optional)

Directions

Roll out the dough into a large rectangle and brush it with Italian dressing.
Top with as many pepperoni as you can fit on the dough.
(optional add whatever your favorite pizza topping are to this)
Sprinkle with cheese and Italian seasoning and roll up tightly, starting with the longest side of dough.
Fold sides under, and place on pan, dough seam side down.
Brush with egg white and sprinkle with garlic powder.
Bake at 425 degrees for 20 minutes.
Let sit for 5 to 10 minutes, then slice and serve.

By then it'll be time to scarf them down without burning your mouth!

*Random Tip~ Put a small amount of water in a glass when you microwave your pizza to keep the crust from getting chewy.

Meatloaf

1 lb. grass fed ground beef (or ground Chicken/ground Turkey to make it healthier)
1 yellow onion, diced
1 roasted red pepper, diced
¼ cup tomato sauce
1 egg
1 tsp dried basil
1 tsp dried thyme
1 tsp dried parsley
A handful of crackers crumbled or bread crumbs
Sea salt & pepper to taste
Olive oil for sautéing

For the Sauce
¼ cup tomato sauce
1 tsp dried basil
1 tsp dried thyme
1 tsp dried parsley
Sea salt & pepper to taste

Directions
Preheat oven to 400 degrees Place a medium skillet over medium heat and add ½ tablespoon of olive oil. Then add onions & roasted red pepper to the pan. Cook until onions are soft & translucent After sautéing onion & pepper – add to a bowl with the rest of the ingredients for meatloaf and mix together with hands. Press ingredients into bread pan and bake 35-40 minutes. When meatloaf is almost done, heat sauce ingredients in pan until slightly bubbly. Let meatloaf cool slightly before adding sauce on top of meatloaf. Top with fresh basil if desired.

~My cooking is fabulous… Even the smoke alarm cheers me on!

Broccoli Frittata

10 Eggs – whisked
½ red onion - diced
1 1/2 cup Broccoli, finely chopped
1 cup Mushrooms, diced
1 tsp garlic powder sea salt and pepper to taste
2 tbsp olive oil

Directions

Heat oil in large pan. Add onions & sauté until they turn brown & caramelize. Add broccoli and mushrooms and sauté for another 4-5 minutes or until the broccoli is tender. Spread the veggie mixture evenly over the bottom of the pan. Whisk the sea salt, pepper, and garlic powder into the eggs and gently pour over the veggie mixture. Cook over low to medium heat for 8-10 minutes or until almost set. Remove from heat. COVER. LET STAND until completely set, approximately 8-10 minutes. Cut into wedges.

Sweet Potato, Kale & Shrimp Skillet

4 tbsps olive oil
1 cup onion, diced   Red pepper flakes, to taste
4 garlic cloves, minced
4 cups sweet potatoes, diced
4 cups fresh shrimp
6 cups trimmed and coarsely chopped kale leaves
Ground black pepper   Salt

Directions

In a saucepan, add the extra virgin olive oil over medium heat. Add onions and red pepper flakes. Cook until onions are soft and golden. Add garlic and cook for about 30 seconds. Add sweet potato and cook until soft. It is about 10-15mins. In case you need, add a few tablespoons of water to help steam the sweet potato. Add shrimp and cook for 2-3 minutes, or until they turn pink. Turn the heat to low and add kale, stirring until wilted. Season to taste with salt and pepper

Thai Curry Ground Beef

Serve on cauliflower rice or brown rice
1 lb lean ground beef
1 leek, sliced thin
2 garlic cloves, minced
1 tsp fresh ginger, raw
1 tbsp red curry paste (or to taste)
1.5 cups canned tomato sauce
1 tsp lime zest
1 tbsp Coconut Aminos
1/2 cup canned light coconut milk
2 tsp lime juice
Directions
*Option 1: Brown the ground beef and then add to the crockpot with the leek, garlic, ginger, red curry paste, tomato sauce, coconut aminos, lime zest. Cook on low for 4 hours. Open the lid and stir in coconut milk and lime juice. Let cook for 15 minutes longer and serve.
*Option 2: Heat a skillet over medium heat and spray with cooking spray. Add the leeks and cook for 4 minutes. Add the beef, garlic, and ginger and cook until beef is no longer pink. Stir in the curry paste and cook for 1 minute. Add the tomato sauce, lime zest, and coconut aminos. Turn the heat down to low and simmer for 10 minutes. Stir in the coconut milk and lime juice. Let cook for 2 more minutes.

Veggie Wraps

Spinach Tortillas
½ cup Veggie Mix (peppers, onions, squash, zucchini)
Cheese shreds
Add fresh spinach.
Directions
Heat large sauté pan to medium heat and prepare surface with light spray of coconut/olive oil. Place tortillas in pan. Heat, then flip. Fill center of tortilla with veggie mix and top with cheese. Cover with lid to allow to melt a bit. Remove from heat, place on a plate and roll into wrap

Old-Fashioned Vegetable Soup

2 bags frozen 'soup' veggies
1 can tomatoes, diced or crushed
1 jar spaghetti sauce
2-4 cups vegetable broth
Salt/pepper to taste
Oregano to taste
1 bay leaf
Brown rice or quinoa, optional

Directions

In large saucepan, add 2 bags frozen mixed veggies (try to avoid mixes with corn), 1 can diced or crushed tomatoes, 1 jar spaghetti sauce and 2-4 cups vegetable broth to your desired consistency.
Season according to taste.
To bring out the full flavor of the veggies and seasoning lest simmer for 30 minutes.
Add salt/pepper/oregano and 1 bay leaf.
If you want to add some healthy grain to this, feel free to add in COOKED brown rice or quinoa.
Quinoa is always your healthiest grain choice.
Want to make it even healthier and use up that leftover lettuce in the fridge? Toss it in it will cook down rather fast and add a bit more texture and color without altering the flavor.

*Random Tip~ A light beer will always make veggie soup taste better!

Give Me All The Sides!!

Need a delicious vegetable idea for tonight? Try this one!
1 and ½ pounds broccoli crowns (roughly 2 heads)
¼ cup extra virgin olive oil
4 garlic cloves, pressed
large pinch of dried red pepper flakes
½ tsp kosher salt
3 tbsp raw, sliced almonds (with or without skin)
2 tbsp freshly squeezed lemon juice
2 – 3 tbsp freshly grated aged pecorino cheese
zest of half a lemon
DIRECTIONS
Preheat the oven to 475 degrees Fahrenheit. Note: The high temperature ensures even and deep caramelization (and extra crispy, flavorful florets!). If your oven runs hot (you can check this by using an oven thermometer) or you prefer less crispy florets, you can reduce the oven temperature by 10 to 15 degrees Fahrenheit and adjust cooking time as necessary.

Line a sheet pan with aluminum foil. Trim any dry, tough ends of broccoli crowns, leaving roughly 2-inches of stalk attached. Slice the broccoli into ½-inch-thick steaks, starting in the center of each broccoli crown and working out to the edges, reserving any small or medium florets that fall off for roasting. Slice any large remaining florets in half lengthwise.

In a large bowl, whisk together the olive oil, pressed garlic, and red pepper flakes. Add the broccoli steaks and toss gently until evenly coated. Arrange the broccoli, cut-side down, on the lined sheet pan, setting them apart slightly. Sprinkle with salt.

Roast the broccoli for 10 to 12 minutes. Remove the pan from the oven, flip the broccoli, and sprinkle the almond slices evenly across the sheet pan. Roast for an additional 8 to 10 minutes, or until the broccoli is evenly caramelized and fork tender, and the almond slices are toasted and golden.

Transfer the broccoli to a platter, toss gently with the lemon juice and top with grated pecorino cheese. Garnish with fresh lemon zest. Serve hot or at room temperature (it also tastes great cold). Leftover broccoli can be stored in an airtight container in the fridge for up to 2 days.

Love those sweet potatoes???

Healthy Chicks Sweet Potato Casserole
2 large sweet potatoes
½ cup apple sauce
1 ½ tbsp coconut oil
1 tsp ground cinnamon
½ tsp sea salt
Pinch of ground nutmeg
1 cup chopped pecans
extra salt and cinnamon for top
Directions
Preheat oven to 450 degrees.
Wrap sweet potatoes in aluminum foil and bake in preheated oven until soft (about 1-1.5 hours)
Remove from oven, cut in half and let cool.
Remove skins and set sweet potatoes aside.
Reduce oven to 375 degrees F.
Add apple sauce and sweet potatoes to your blender and blend until smooth
Add melted coconut oil, cinnamon, salt and nutmeg and blend until combined.
Transfer to a 9" baking dish and sprinkle the top with pecans, cinnamon and sea salt (sprinkled)
Bake at 375 for 25-30 minutes until potatoes begin to slightly bubble and topping is lightly

Roasted Broccoli

Preheat oven to 425.

Remove bulk of stems from 1 head of broccoli. Prepare cookie sheet with coconut or olive oil spray and place broccoli evenly on pan.

Place a couple pats of butter across the top. Sprinkle with salt/pepper and garlic salt. Roast for 8-10 minutes and serve.

Mexican Style Sweet Potato

2 sweet potatoes
1 tablespoon extra-virgin olive oil
½ white onion, diced
½ red pepper, diced
1 garlic clove, minced
½ tsp sea salt
1 lime, juiced
1 can black beans

Directions

Extra-virgin olive oil Parsley, chopped. Pop the sweet potatoes into the oven and bake at 400 degrees Fahrenheit for one hour. Remove from the oven and slice each potato lengthwise.

Scoop out the insides so that there is only a thin layer remaining lining the edges. Set aside.

Heat olive oil in a frying pan over medium heat, and cook the chopped vegetables until tender, about seven minutes. Season with salt to taste. Drain and rinse the black beans and add to the frying pan along with the lime juice. While the bean and vegetable combo is cooking, mash the mixture with the edge of a fork to break up the beans. Add the cooked sweet potato insides to the bean mixture and mix until thoroughly combined.

Stuff each potato with the bean mixture and serve with a drizzle of extra-virgin olive oil and chopped parsley.

Scrumptious Roasted Vegetables Recipe

1 medium eggplant quartered and sliced into ½ inch pieces
1 large carrot sliced into ½ inch pieces on the diagonal
2 medium red onions cut into ½ inch strips
1 red bell pepper cut into ½ inch strips
1 yellow bell pepper cut into ½ inch strips
2 medium squash, quartered and sliced into ½ inch pieces
1 butternut squash peeled, quartered and sliced into 1 inch pieces
15 Brussels sprouts cut in half or whole
1 zucchini sliced into ½ inch rounds
**For the dressing:
½ cup good quality extra virgin olive oil
2 tbsp good quality balsamic vinegar not overly sweet
2 tsp Dijon mustard
2 tsp finely chopped fresh thyme
1 Tbsp finely chopped fresh Italian basil
5 garlic cloves pressed
1 tsp freshly ground black pepper
1 tsp kosher salt
½ tsp freshly ground black pepper optional
½ tsp kosher salt plus more to taste

Directions

Preheat oven to 450F.

Line a large, 15x21-inch baking sheet with parchment paper and set aside. If you are using smaller baking sheets you will need to roast the vegetables in two batches or on two baking sheets.

Prepare the dressing by whisking the olive oil, vinegar, Dijon mustard, basil, thyme, garlic, pepper and salt in a small bowl, until well combined.

Place the vegetables in a large bowl, big enough to accommodate all the veggies and still having some head space left to allow tossing. Pour dressing all over the vegetables and toss well to coat the veggies with an even layer of the dressing.

Transfer the vegetables onto the baking dish and spread evenly. Sprinkle additional salt and pepper on top.

Bake on top rack for about 35 minutes (slightly firmer) to 45 minutes Start checking at 30 minutes as different ovens bake differently. Serve the roasted vegetables immediately.

Veggie Fried Rice

2 cups cooked brown rice
2 tbsp olive oil
2 tbsp soy sauce
1-2 cups baby spinach, tightly-packed
½ cup onions, diced
½ broccoli, diced
½ cup carrots, diced

Directions

Sesame seeds, optional Salt/pepper/garlic powder to taste. Toss in cashews or chickpeas for added protein, optional

Heat skillet to medium heat and add 2 tbsp olive oil.

Saute onions, broccoli & carrots and any other desired veggies under tender. Add spinach for final few minutes.

Add cooked brown rice.

Add soy sauce and sesame seeds (optional). If mixture is getting dry, add a splash of veggie broth.

*Random Tip~ The numbers on a toaster are the number of minutes you want to toast for, not the degree of toasty-ness. My whole life has been a sham!!!

Twice Baked Potato Casserole With Bacon

2 large baking potatoes
½ pound lean bacon
¾ cup shredded mild Cheddar cheese
½ cup sour cream
¼ cup milk
2 tbsp unsalted butter, melted
1 tsp dried chives
½ tsp salt
½ tsp ground black pepper
½ tsp garlic powder
¾ cup shredded mild Cheddar cheese

Directions

Preheat oven to 400 degrees F (200 degrees C). Grease a 9×13-inch casserole dish.
Poke a few holes into each potato using a toothpick.
Bake potatoes in the preheated oven until fully cooked, about 1 hour. Cool for about 15 minutes.
Place the bacon in a large skillet and cook over medium-high heat, turning occasionally, until evenly browned, about 10 minutes. Drain the bacon slices on paper towels and crumble.
Cut a thin slice from one side of each potato; carefully scoop out the flesh and transfer to a bowl. Discard skins.
Mix 3/4 cup Cheddar cheese, sour cream, milk, butter, chives, salt, black pepper, and garlic powder with potatoes. Spread potato mixture into prepared casserole dish; top with 3/4 cup Cheddar cheese and crumbled bacon.
Bake in preheated oven until just bubbling, 10 to 15 minutes. Cool for at least 5 minutes before serving.

*Random Tip~ "Nigglywiggly" is the actual name of the little paper flag thingy sticking out of the top of the Hershey's kisses!

Sweet Potato Fries

Olive Oil, for tossing
5 sweet potatoes, peeled and sliced into 1/4-inch long slices, then ¼ wide inch strips
2 tsp salt
½ tsp pepper
½ tsp garlic powder
½ tsp paprika
Directions
Preheat oven to 450 degrees F.
Line a sheet tray with parchment. In a large bowl toss sweet potatoes with just enough oil to coat. Sprinkle with House Seasoning and paprika. Spread the sweet potatoes in single layer on prepared baking sheet, being sure not to overcrowd. Bake until sweet potatoes are tender and golden brown, turning occasionally, about 20 minutes.

Vampire Baked Garlic Parmesan Fries

1 tbsp garlic, minced very fine
2 tbsp olive oil
2 large baking potatoes, 12 ounces each or 1½ pounds total
Salt and pepper, to taste
2 tbsp parmesan cheese
½ tsp garlic powder, or to taste
Directions
Preheat oven to 450 degrees. Line 1 baking sheet with foil and coat a baking sheet with cooking spray.
Cut the potatoes lengthwise in half and in half again. Cut each piece into ¼-½ inch thick strips. Place on baking sheet and toss with olive oil and garlic. Use your hands to evenly coat. Spread the potatoes evenly over the entire pan. Season with a little salt and black pepper. Bake uncovered in the center of the oven until tender crisp and golden brown, about 20-25 minutes on each side. Baking time will vary depending on how thick your pieces are and your oven. Set your timer for 20 minutes and check.
Remove from oven and sprinkle with Parmesan cheese and a little garlic powder. Add a little more salt and pepper, if desired.

Brussels Sprouts In Garlic Butter

15 Brussels sprouts, halved lengthwise
1 ½ tbsp butter
1 ½ tbsp olive oil
3 cloves garlic, smashed with the flat of a knife
freshly grated parmesan cheese (optional)
salt and pepper

Melt butter and olive oil in a medium skillet (over medium-high heat) until butter is foamy.
Reduce heat to medium, add smashed garlic and cook until lightly browned.
Remove garlic and discard.
Add sprouts cut side down, cover, and cook without stirring on medium-low heat 10-15 minutes or until tender when pierced with a knife.
The cut side of the sprouts should get nice and browned, with a nutty, buttery flavor enhanced by garlic.
Top with freshly grated parmesan and salt & pepper to taste.

Cauliflower Rice

¾ head cauliflower (about 6 cups riced)
⅛ cup minced onion
1 tbsp Extra Virgin Olive Oil

Directions

Roughly chop cauliflower and place in a food processor. (Note: Do not overfill the food processor, in order to properly 'rice' cauliflower it needs room) Pulse cauliflower in a food processor until it is about the texture of rice. If necessary work in batches. Heat olive oil in pan over medium heat. Once oil is heated add onion and sauté until onion is soft and translucent. Add in riced cauliflower and cook, stirring occasionally for about 10-20 minutes or until soft

Time to wake up food!

Egg Cupcakes

10-12 eggs whisked well
Add all your favorite omelet items
Directions
Preheat oven to 350 degrees & grease 2 muffin pans with olive oil. Whisk all eggs in large bowl. Add all your favorites & then add to your egg mixture.
Mix all together well & then fill muffin pans using ¼ measuring cup
Bake for 20-25 minutes or until eggs are set in the middle.

Apple Walnut Oatmeal Breakfast Bowl

½ of a cup uncooked Oatmeal
1 Green Apple (cored and diced)
2½ cups of Water
2 teaspoons Brown Sugar
1 teaspoon Cinnamon
1/3 cup Walnut Halves
Directions
Dice a green apple. In a small saucepan and water. Bring to boil, uncovered, over medium-high heat.
Reduce heat add oatmeal and simmer for 15-20 minutes, stirring occasionally, until nearly all the water has been absorbed. Remove saucepan from heat. Stir cinnamon in.

*Random Tip~ Keep Bananas fresh longer by wrapping the vine part with seran wrap.

Avocado Toast EGG-IN-A-HOLE

The perfect 5-minute breakfast to make the one you love!
Whole grain toast with mashed avocado, eggs over easy and a few dashes of hot sauce
5 ingredients, 5 minutes to make, doesn't get better than that!

1 slice whole wheat or whole grain bread
1 oz avocado
olive oil spray
1 large egg
Kosher salt and freshly ground black pepper
hot sauce (optional)

Directions
With a heart-shaped cutter or the rim of a glass, press a hole in the center of the slice of bread.
Mash the avocado with a fork and season with salt and pepper.

Heat a skillet over medium-low heat and spray with oil. Place the bread and the cut-out piece on the skillet and crack the egg straight into the center of the hole.
Cook until the egg sets on the bottom, about 1 minute, season with salt and pepper and flip over with a spatula, season with salt and pepper the other side.
Cook the other side until the yolk is to your liking, I prefer mine soft.

Remove and top with avocado and hot sauce if desired.
Also great with Everything Bagel seasoning!
(This shit is like red hot or Ranch! It goes on everything!)

Pumpkin-Apple-Almond Overnight Oats (Trent approved)

½ cup oats
1 cup of vanilla almond milk
2 tbsp of organic pumpkin puree
2 tbsp of applesauce (or/and microwave a couple slices of granny smith apple and mash)
1 tsp of chia seeds
1 tsp of flax/hemp seeds
¼ cup chopped green apple slices
¼ cup of raw almonds
Directions
Nutmeg, Cinnamon, and Pumpkin Pie Spice (add to your preference)
Mix all ingredients together in a mason jar.
Place in the fridge to sit overnight.
In the morning, eat it cold or throw it in the microwave for 1-2 minutes if you prefer to enjoy it warm (I like this over eating them cold), but you can enjoy them either way.
Will stay on the fridge up to 6 days

Basic Bitch Overnight Oats :)

½ cup oats
½ cup of vanilla almond milk
1 tsp of chia seeds
Mix all ingredients together in a mason jar.. Place in the fridge to sit overnight.
In the morning, throw it in the microwave for 1-2 minutes if you prefer to enjoy it warm.
I like these cold great for camping, road tips or busy mornings.
Will stay on the fridge up to 6 days

Snack Time!!

Drunk Night Crescent Sausage Bites
1 lb hot sausage (pork or turkey)
1 (8 oz.) package cream cheese
2 packages crescent rolls
Dash salt & ground black pepper
Directions
In a saute pan, brown sausage, drain.
Add a dash of salt and pepper. Blend in cream cheese until the cream cheese is melted.
Unroll one package of crescent rolls and place on a baking sheet.
With your fingers, gently press the seams together to seal them.
Spread the sausage mixture evenly over the crescent roll dough, leaving a ½ inch border along the edges.
Unroll the remaining package of crescent rolls and place on top of the sausage mixture.
Press the edges together to seal. Gently press the seams together.
Bake at 375 degrees for about 20 minutes, or until crescent roll dough is golden brown.
Cut into small squares and serve.
(A pizza cutter makes really quick and easy work of the cutting.)

***Random Tip~ If you place a ripe banana next to a green tomato for 24 hours. The tomato will ripen due to the ethylene gas produced by bananas!**

Hummus

3 cans of chickpeas
5 cloves roasted garlic or 1-2 cloves fresh
4 tbsp lemon juice
1 tsp salt
¼ tsp black pepper
½ c water or other liquid (placed in bottom of blender)
1-2 tbsp Extra virgin olive oil (texture to taste)
Directions
Strain water from boiled chickpeas. Add ingredients into a food processor or blender. Be sure to add liquid first. Process until smooth. (NOTE: if using a blender, if needed stop and scrape to mix well. The Hummus can be really thick and bind up in the blade of a blender.) Transfer to a container with a lid and drizzle with toppings. Refrigerate and enjoy over the course of 1 week.

My Famous Salsa (hot)

7 roma tomatoes
1 small white onion peeled and roughly chopped
1 - 2 jalapeno peppers seeded and chopped
3 cloves garlic chopped
1 ½ tsp ground cumin or to taste
1 tsps salt or to taste
1 - 2 handfuls cilantro I prefer 2
About 3 tbsp lime juice
1 tablespoon of red wine vinegar
Add all ingredients to food processor pulse to desired texture.
Transfer to airtight container and let sit in the refrigerator for a couple of hours or 1 day for best flavor. Will last up to 1 week.
Serve with tortilla chips and enjoy!

Black Bean Dip

1 can (organic) canned black beans
1 tsp cumin
½ tsp paprika (optional)
½ tsp coriander (optional)
2 t olive oil
¼ cup water
Juice of ¼ lemon
1 tsp sea salt
Directions
Drain and rinse black beans well. Add all ingredients to a food processor and blitz for 2 minutes. Store in a tightly sealed container for up to 3 days in the fridge.

Fresh Tomato Salsa

1 small onion
½ cup fresh cilantro
½ tsp salt
2 garlic cloves-peeled
2 tbsp fresh lemon juice
2 cups grape tomatoes
Directions
Combine ingredients in the manual food processor except tomatoes. Process lightly then add tomatoes and pulse to desired consistency.

Fresh Pico De Gallo

Equal Parts Diced Garden Tomatoes and Diced White Onion
Leaves of 2 bunches of fresh cilantro
3-5 minced jalapeño peppers
Juice of 4-5 fresh limes
Sea salt & Pepper to Taste
Gently, combine and it's all ready!

Guacamole

4-5 Avocados mashed
2-3 cloves garlic, minced
½ large red onion, diced
1 jalapeno diced (seeds removed)
Small handful of cilantro, roughly chopped Juice of 1 lime
½ tsp or so of salt and pepper
1 medium tomatoes diced
Mix all together, adding tomato at the end

Guacamole Light

In a food processor chop: ½ red onion
Large handful of cilantro Juice of 1 lime
Salt to taste
1 jalapeno
Add mixture to large bowl and mix with 5-6 avocados. Add additional lime and salt to taste.

Kale Chips

1 Bunch Kale
2-3 tbsp Olive Oil Salt (to taste)
Garlic Powder (to taste)
Directions
Cut leaves from stem and tear into chip sized pieces. Wash leaves. Dry leaves by placing 1 layer on half a kitchen towel and folding opposite half on top to gently remove excess water. Put leaves in a bowl and add olive oil and seasonings.
Place leaves on baking sheets in a single layer (for 1 bunch of kale uses about 2 baking sheets).
Bake at 350 F for 7-10 minutes. Remove trays from oven and use spatula to flip chips over. Return to oven and bake for another 3-7 minutes until chips are dehydrated. Remove from oven and let cool. Chips will crisp as they cool.

Egg Roll in a Bowl

1 lb Beef or Chicken- sliced
½ Head Cabbage, shredded (3-4 cups)
1 cup Carrot, shredded.
5 cloves Garlic, minced
1 tsp sesame seed oil
1 tsp ginger
½ cup Coconut Aminos Green Onion, sliced
1 tsp Apple Cider Vinegar Sesame Seeds (optional)
Directions
In a large skillet, brown Ground Beef or Chicken
In a small bowl, whisk together sesame seed oil, vinegar, garlic, coconut aminos and ginger, set aside.
Add the cabbage and carrot to the skillet and toss to combine. Stir in the dressing mixture.
Cover and cook until the vegetables are soft, about 15 minutes. Garnish with green onion and sesame seeds

Dill Salmon (w/Stir-fried Veggies and Brown Rice)

Salmon
Dill
Put the frozen package of salmon in the fridge the morning you want to cook it and it will defrost safely.
When you are ready to cook, season the fillets with a little bit of dill and fresh lemon or lime. Use a nonstick pan for.
I heated up some olive oil, then I put the salmon fillets in "upside down" (always purchase the salmon with skin on), cover the pan and cook for about 5 minutes, then flip the salmon and cook for another 5 minutes, then flip the salmon and cook for another 5 minutes, on medium to high heat.
This is wonderful with some stir-fried vegetables and brown rice.

Mini Eggplant Pizzas

1 eggplant (8 oz, 9-10" long)
1 tsp salt
2 tbsp olive oil
2 tbsp dried Italian seasoning
10 large basil leaves, cut in strips (optional)
⅓ cup Parmesan (optional)
⅓ cup mozzarella shredded
Pinch of Crushed red pepper flakes (optional)
1 jar Spaghetti Sauce (Muir Glen Italian Herb)

Cut off both ends of the eggplant; then cut it into ¾ inch thick slices (trying to make them the same thickness!)

Put the eggplant pieces on a double layer of paper towels and sprinkle both sides generously with salt.

Let the eggplant sit with the salt on it for about 30 minutes to draw out the liquid. (After the eggplant sits for 15 minutes, turn on the oven to 375F/190C.) After 30 minutes, wipe the eggplant dry with paper towels (this also removes most of the salt.) Spray a roasting sheet with olive oil or non-stick spray, lay eggplant slices on, brush the tops of the eggplant with olive oil, and sprinkle with dried Italian seasoning.

Roast the eggplant about 25 minutes but "not so long that the slices become mushy and lose their shape."

While the eggplant roasts, thinly slice the fresh basil leaves (if using) and combined freshly grated Parmesan and low-fat mozzarella blend.

After 25 minutes or when eggplant pieces are done, remove eggplant from the oven and turn the oven setting to broil.

Spread a few tablespoons of sauce on the top of each eggplant slice, sprinkle with thin basil slices (if using) and top with a generous amount of cheese.

Put pizzas under the broiler until the cheese is melted and slightly browned. (This took 6-7 minutes using a toaster oven and in a more powerful broiler it would probably only take a few minutes.)

Serve hot, with red pepper flakes to sprinkle on pizza if desired.

Crockpot Goodies

Easy Crockpot Chicken and Dumplings
3 boneless, skinless chicken breasts
2 tbsp butter
2 cans cream of chicken soup
1 (14.5 oz) can of chicken broth
½ onion diced
1 tbsp dried parsley
½ can Grands flaky refrigerator biscuits (I used a whole can, I like dumplings)
Directions
Place Chicken breasts in crock pot and top with butter.
Add 2 cans of cream of chicken soup
Add chicken broth
Add diced onions and dried parsley
Cover and cook on high for 4-5 hours or low 8-9 hours
Once cooked shred the chicken
Cut biscuits into 9 pieces
Add biscuits to the soup and stir
Cover and cook on high for another hour
Serve warm and enjoy!
note:
Made it yesterday, it was great! Cooked up everything in the crockpot except the biscuits. After it was finished in the crockpot I moved it to a pot and added some peas and carrots for a little color, brought the pot to an easy boil then flattened the biscuits out and cut them into some half dollar size

Slow Cooker Whole Chicken Recipe with Lemon

ground cumin
paprika
turmeric
cayenne pepper
(all to taste)
1 whole lemon
One whole chicken
1 chopped onion
5 cloves garlic, chopped
½ cup chopped cilantro
1 pound carrots, chopped
2 red bell peppers, chopped
1 can fire roasted crushed tomatoes

Directions

In a small bowl, mix together all the spices and juice from lemon (reserving the lemon rind). Apply the spice mixture generously all over the inside and outside of the bird. Stuff the cavity of the chicken with half of the onions, half of the garlic and half of the cilantro. Place the remaining onions, garlic and cilantro, carrots, peppers and tomatoes in the bottom of slow cooker. Place the chicken on top of vegetables.

Cover and cook on low for about 6 hours or on high for approximately 3 ½ to 4 hours, or until the meat pulls easily away from the bones.

Serve warm on a bed of fresh spinach, over rice or with a side salad.

*Random Tip~ Storing potatoes with apple will keep them from sprouting longer.

Tomato & Roasted Red Pepper Soup

2 carrots, peeled and chopped
2 celery stalks, chopped
1 onion, chopped
4 garlic cloves, minced
72 oz. can whole tomatoes with juices
14 oz. roasted red peppers in water
4 cups vegetable broth
¼ cup fresh basil
1 bay leaf Salt and pepper
Directions
Add everything to the slow cooker. Cook on low for 8 hours

2 Bean Chili

28oz can crushed tomatoes (or diced, based on preference)
1 can kidney beans
1 can pinto beans
1 onion, diced
2 tbsp chili powder
1 tbsp fresh minced garlic
½ tsp salt
½ tsp black pepper
½ tsp oregano
½ tsp cumin
½ tsp cayenne pepper
½ tsp paprika
2 cups water
2 cups cooked quinoa (or brown rice, optional)
½ avocado, sliced (optional) If desired
Directions
Cook quinoa (or brown rice) according to package instructions. In large 2 qt covered pot, add all ingredients, heat through and serve it up! This is SO good and SO easy. We serve it over cooked brown rice. Optional: Top with avocado slices or DF cheddar cheese shreds.

Turkey Chili

1 lb ground turkey, browned
1 28 oz. can diced or crushed tomatoes
1 can kidney beans
½ onion, diced
2 tbsp chili powder
1 tbsp fresh minced garlic
½ tsp salt
½ tsp black pepper
½ tsp oregano
½ tsp cumin
½ tsp cayenne pepper
½ tsp paprika
2 cups water
2 cups cooked brown rice

Directions

Cook rice according to package instructions. In large skillet brown turkey and onions together until done. In large 2 quart add remaining ingredients, heat through and add turkey/onion to and simmer for 20 minutes.

Slow Cooker White Chicken Chili

2.5 lbs. boneless skinless chicken breast
1 onion, minced
4 garlic cloves, minced
2 jalapeno (seeded for less heat), diced
2 poblano peppers (seeded for less heat), diced
½ cup cilantro, chopped
2 tsp cumin
1 tsp oregano
6 cups low sodium chicken broth
Salt and pepper to taste
1 lime

Directions

Thinly slice and dice chicken. Add everything to the slow cooker and cook on low for 4 hours.. Add back in and serve.

Slow Cooker Brown Sugar Chicken

3 pounds of chicken thighs, skin removed
½ tsp of kosher salt, or to taste
¼ tsp of freshly cracked black pepper, or to taste
¼ tsp of Creole or Cajun seasoning (like Slap Ya Mama), or to taste
¼ tsp of garlic powder, or to taste
½ cup of light brown sugar, packed
1 (6 ounce) can of pineapple juice
⅓ cup of soy sauce
2 tbsp of cornstarch
2 tbsp of water

Directions

Remove skin from chicken & season lightly with salt, pepper, Cajun seasoning and garlic powder. Pat seasoning into chicken and place into the slow cooker.

Whisk together the brown sugar, pineapple juice & soy sauce; pour around chicken. Cover and cook on low for 5 to 6 hours, depending on the size of the chicken. Use a wide spatula to remove the chicken from the slow cooker to a platter & loosely tent with aluminum foil; set aside to prepare the glaze.

Turn cooker to high until mixture comes to a boil, or transfer to a saucepan on the stovetop. Whisk together the water & cornstarch until there are no lumps. Slowly stir into the boiling sauce until fully incorporated & continue boiling for about 3 to 4 minutes or until mixture thickens.

Remove from heat and let rest for a moment.

Brush the sauce over each chicken thigh & serve the remaining sauce at the table.

Note: I also added a few grinds of Rachel Ray's Perfect Poultry seasoning to the chicken, which contains sea salt, pepper, onion, sage, rosemary & thyme. I also used low sodium soy sauce.

The Good Shit, Desserts!!

Apple Crisp
5 Granny Smith Apples, peeled, cored, diced
½ cup coconut oil, melted (or butter)
1 cup chopped nuts (optional)
1 cup rolled oats
4 tbsp brown sugar
¾ tsp salt
2 tbsp cinnamon
Directions
Preheat oven to 350 degrees.. Peel, core and slice apples. Place apples 11" baker. Warm coconut oil in a pan, if not already melted.
Chop nuts, if using them. Add nuts, coconut oil, oatmeal, brown sugar, salt & cinnamon into a large bowl. Mix well, Add honey to taste. mix till it all gets crumbly.
Sprinkle mixture evenly over apples. Be sure to cover apples completely, to seal in the juices and keep the apple slices moist.
Bake 35-45 minutes or until apples are tender and crumbs are golden brown.
Serve warm, ice cream :)

Banana Cookies
2 Bananas
1 cup oats
2 tbsp peanut butter
Mix all together
Bake for 10- 15 minutes at 350 degrees

OMG Lemon Brownies

½ cup unsalted butter, softened
¾ cup flour
2 eggs, large
2 tbsp lemon zest
2 tbsp lemon juice
¾ cup granulated sugar
¼ tsp sea salt

**Tart Lemon Glaze

4 tbsp lemon juice
8 tsp lemon zest
1 cup icing sugar

Directions
Preheat the oven to 350 degrees.
Grease an 8×8 inch baking dish with butter and set aside.
Zest and juice two lemons and set aside.
In the bowl of an electric mixer fitted with the paddle attachment, beat the flour, sugar, salt, and softened butter until combined.
In a separate bowl, whisk together eggs, lemon zest, and lemon juice until combined.
Pour it into the flour mixture and beat for 2 mins at medium speed until smooth and creamy.
Pour into baking dish and bake for 23-25 mins, should turn golden around the edges.
Allow to cool completely before glazing. Do not overbake, or the bars will dry.
Filter the powdered sugar and whisk with lemon zest and juice.
Spread the glaze over the brownies with a rubber spatula and let glaze set.
Cut into bars and serve

~These are FREAKING AMAZING!!!!

Country Apple Fritter Bread

⅓ cup light brown sugar
1 tsp ground cinnamon
⅔ cup white sugar
½ cup butter, softened
2 eggs
1 ½ tsp vanilla extract
1 ½ cups all-purpose flour
1 ¾ tsp baking powder
½ cup milk
2 Apples, peeled and chopped (any kind)
Directions

**Old-Fashioned Creme Glaze

½ cup powdered sugar
2 tbsp of milk or cream
Directions

Preheat oven to 350°F. Use a 9×5-inch loaf pan and spray with non-stick spray or line with foil and spray with non-stick spray to get out easily for slicing. Mix brown sugar and cinnamon together in a bowl. Set aside.

In another medium-sized bowl, beat white sugar and butter together using an electric mixer until smooth and creamy. Beat in eggs, 1 at a time, until blended then add in vanilla extract.

Combine & whisk flour and baking powder together in another bowl and add into creamed butter mixture and stir until blended. Mix milk into batter until smooth.

Pour half the batter into prepared loaf pan; add half the apple mixture, then half the brown sugar/cinnamon mixture. Lightly pat apple mixture into batter.

Pour the remaining batter over apple layer and top with remaining apple mixture, then the remaining brown sugar/cinnamon mixture.

Lightly pat apples into batter; swirl brown sugar mixture through apples using knife or spoon. Bake in preheated oven until a toothpick inserted in the center of the loaf comes out clean, approximately 50-60 minutes.

To make glaze, mix powdered sugar and milk or cream together until well mixed.

Let cool for about 15 minutes before drizzling with glaze.

Enjoy! Don't eat the whole pan....OK! Go ahead!

Southern Pecan Praline Cake

1 box Betty Crocker butter pecan cake mix
16 oz. can Betty Crocker Coconut Pecan Frosting
4 large eggs
¾ cup canola or coconut oil
1 cup half-and-half for increased flavor instead of water
½ cup chopped pecans
Butter Pecan Glaze
14 oz. can sweetened condensed milk
3 tbsp butter
½ cup chopped pecans

Directions

Preheat oven to 350°.
Grease or spray a 9×13 baking dish with cooking spray.
In a mixing bowl, combine all the cake ingredients except for the chopped pecans. Mix well.
Add chopped pecans and stir to combine.
Pour batter into prepared baking dish.
Bake for about 40-50 minutes or until toothpick inserted in center comes out clean.

**Butter Pecan Glaze:

In a small saucepan over medium heat, melt butter.
Add condensed milk and stir.
Heat thoroughly, then add chopped pecans.
Stir again to combine and remove from heat.
Spoon sauce over individual slices of cake or spread over the entire cake (much easier).

**Notes:

The Coconut Pecan Frosting is included in the cake batter.
It is NOT an icing for the top of the cake nor included in the sauce.
The cake took 50 minutes to bake, although the original instructions said 30-40 minutes for a 9×13" pan and 50 minutes for a bundt pan.

Protein Balls

2 cup almond butter
1 ¼ cup honey or liquid stevia (sweetener of choice)
1 cup vanilla protein powder (4 scoops)
1 cup chocolate protein powder (4 scoops)
2 cup steel cut oats
½ cup chia seeds
½ cup flax seeds

Directions

Melt nut butter and sweetner together in medium saucepan. Then add the rest of the ingredients. Mix well until all protein is mixed in. Form into 1 inch balls and refrigerate.

Lemon Almond Protein Balls

Melt and mix together:
2 cup nut butter
1 ⅛ cup honey or liquid stevia (sweetener of choice)
Mix in
2 cup Vanilla protein powder
1 tsp Vanilla
1 tsp Lemon extract
Zest of 2 lemons
1 ⅛ cups sliced almonds
½ cups rice puffs

Mix together and form into balls. Place in fridge to set.

Very Berry Popsicle

1 cup raspberries
1 cup blackberries
1 cup strawberries
1 cup blueberries
Honey or liquid stevia to taste if needed 2 tbsp lemon juice

Blend together in blender. Pour into popsicle molds. Freeze and enjoy

Chocolate Chip Cheesecake Cookies

1 ¼ cup all purpose flour
¼ cup cornstarch
½ tsp of baking powder
¼ cup unsalted butter, room temperature
4 oz cream cheese, room temperature
1 large egg
1 tbsp milk
½ tsp vanilla extract
1 ¼ cup powdered sugar
5-6 tsp mini chocolate chip

Directions

In a medium bowl combine flour, cornstarch and baking powder. Leave aside.
In a large bowl mix butter and cream cheese, with an electric mixer on medium speed, until it is fine and creamy.
Add an egg, milk and vanilla extract and continue mixing.
Then, add powdered sugar and mix some more until the mixture is fluffy.
Put in dry ingredients and mix until you get fine dough.
Finally, add mini chocolate chips and stir well. Leave in fridge for an hour.
Preheat the oven to 375 F. Line two baking sheets with parchment paper.
Take the dough out of the fridge. Shape it into balls (24-26 balls).
Place them in the baking sheets, 1.5 inch apart. Flatten the balls using your hands or some firm object.
Sprinkle some mini chocolate chips, if you wish. Bake for 10 minutes.
Take them out of the oven and leave to cool on the baking sheets for a few minutes.
Transfer them to a wire rack to cool down completely.Notes: Store them in well sealed container, at room temperature, for about three days.

A Few of MY FAV Homemade Healthy Pantry Options

Almond Milk
1 cup almonds
3-4 C water
1 tsp vanilla (if vanilla flavor is desired)
Directions
Soak almonds overnight in enough water to cover them. (Note: This step is optional. Some people are irritated by an enzyme found in raw almonds. If your stomach is not irritated by raw almonds then you can skip this step.) Place almonds and water in a blender and starting on the lowest setting work your way up to the highest setting and allow to blend for about 1 minute. Pour contents of blender through a strainer bag into another container. (Strainer bags can easily be found at your local hardware store in the painting section for a couple of bucks. You're looking for paint strainer bags, much less expensive than "nut milk straining bags" found at fancy food stores.) Squeeze the pulp in the bag to remove all of the delicious 'milk'. (Note: Save the pulp and make almond flour out of it.) Transfer almond milk to a container and place in refrigerator. Use within 2-3 days. Note: For a thicker, richer almond milk use less water and/or more almonds.

*Random Tip~ When you buy a container of cake frosting from the store. Whip it with your mixer for a few minutes. You can double it in size, frost more cupcakes ect. With the same amount and eat less sugar per serving!

Almond Butter

3 cup raw or roasted almonds
1 tbsp coconut oil
½ tsp sea salt

Directions

Place almonds in a food processor and turn on.
(Warning: The noise that initially hits your ears is hideous. You will think your food processor is breaking, but it's not. It's okay; almonds are just tough little nuts).
Walk away... Seriously, this takes a little while so if you need to go do something; it's okay to walk away. If you stand there and watch it the entire time you may go crazy.
Once almonds are in a liquid/paste like state add coconut oil and salt if desired.
IMPORTANT NOTE: Making Almond butter is a patience game. The almonds go through many stages before they reach the coveted 'butter' stage. Those stages look as follows: ground up to a fine flour and sticking to the sides/top of the food processor starting to stick together and resemble a paste clumped together and slowing moving as a blob through the food processor formed into a ball and quickly moving around the food processor (this is the stage most people quit at and it's ok here, but nothing compared to the next stage... believe me, it's worth the wait.)
As the blender is running seemingly liquid.

The heat and friction from the blender magically transforms and extracts the oils and goodness from the almonds and this state is where the 'liquid gold' is.

Seriously, so good. Enjoy!

Cauliflower Tortillas
(for wraps/pizza crusts)
2 cup packed cauliflower rice
2 eggs
Salt/pepper to taste
Directions
Preheat oven to 375 F.
Measure out cauliflower rice and place in kitchen towel or cheesecloth and squeeze all excess liquid out.
(NOTE: The more liquid squeezed out the better)
See note again just to make sure all the liquid is out VIP
Place drained cauliflower rice, eggs, and salt and pepper in a bowl and mix until combined.
Prepare a baking sheet with parchment paper.
Spoon tortilla mixture onto baking sheet and make small flat circles the size of desired tortillas.
Bake for 12 minutes.
Remove pan from oven and use spatula to flip over tortillas. Bake for another 8-12 minutes.
Remove from oven when tortillas are soft and cooked through.
At this point the tortillas can be stored in a sealed container in the refrigerator until ready for use or finish the recipe immediately.
Preheat skillet on stove to medium-high heat.
Place tortillas in skillet one at a time and brown on both sides
(this step is important as it brings out a nice flavor in the tortillas).

Serve immediately with your favorite fillings.

Salad Dressings, Sauces & Seasonings

Ranch Seasoning
2 tbsp dried parsley
1 ½ tsp dried dill weed
2 tsp garlic powder
2 tsp onion powder
2 tsp dried onion flakes
1 tsp ground black pepper
1 tsp dried chives
1 tsp salt Mix all spices together and store in an airtight container. Most recipes will use 1-2 tbsp of seasoning

Ranch Dip
1(13oz) can full-fat coconut milk (make sure it has guar gum in ingredient list) or sour cream
2 ¼ tsp lemon juice
¼ tsp sea salt
1 ½ tbsp Ranch Seasoning

Chili Powder
¼ cup ground chili - ancho is best, but paprika can do in a pinch, smoked paprika is great if available
2 tbsp ground cumin
2 tbsp dried Mexican oregano
1 tsp cayenne (More or less depending on heat preference)

Mississippi Comeback Sauce
This sauce is seriously addictive! If you haven't tried this yet you need to make this ASAP!

This sauce can be used for so many yummy foods! Try Comeback Sauce with; onion Rings, fries, sweet potato fries, hamburgers, veggies

Makes a pint jar full.
1 cup mayonnaise
¼ cup ketchup
¼ cup chili sauce
1 tsp Dijon mustard
1 tsp onion powder
1 tsp garlic powder
2 teaspoons Worcestershire sauce
½ teaspoon ground black pepper
½ teaspoon Tabasco sauce
¼ cup olive oil
Juice of one lemon
Mix all ingredients well and store in refrigerator overnight. It needs to sit to let the flavors become "acquainted".
Use on EVERYTHING (except cheerios)!

Taco Seasoning (you will never buy store seasoning again:)
¼ cup chili powder
1 tsp garlic powder
1 tsp onion powder
1 tsp crushed red pepper flakes
1 tsp dried oregano
2 tbsp paprika
2 tbsp ground cumin
1 ½ tbsp sea salt
1 ½ tbsp black pepper
Mix all spices together and store in airtight container.

Italian Seasoning

1 tsp garlic powder
1 tbsp onion powder
1 tbsp powdered stevia
1 tbsp dried parsley
2 tbsp oregano
1 tsp white pepper
¼ tsp thyme
1 tsp basil
¼ tsp celery seed
Mix all spices together and store in airtight container.

Roasted Garlic

1 fist garlic
2 tbsp olive oil
Directions
Preheat oven to 375 degrees. Cut top off of garlic fist. Place in small oven proof dish. Pour oil over garlic and cover with tinfoil. Bake for 45 minutes or until cloves are soft. Remove from oven and let cool. Pop/squeeze cloves out of paper.

Mayonnaise

1 egg yolk
1 tbsp lemon juice
½ tbsp mustard
¾ cup oil (grape seed or avocado)
Sea salt, to taste
Directions
Place the egg yolk in the bowl of a food processor and add the lemon juice and mustard. Season with salt, to taste. Turn the machine on and very slowly start to drizzle in the oil. Drip, drip, drip until the mixture starts to look like mayonnaise, then a slow steady stream of oil can be added. Cook's Note: If the mayonnaise is too thick add a few drops of water or if it is not thick enough, with the machine running, add a little more oil.

Caesar Dressing

2 cloves garlic, minced
1 tsp fish sauce (may need more depending on taste)
2 tbsp freshly squeezed lemon juice, from one lemon
1 tsp mustard
1 cup mayonnaise
¼ tsp salt
¼ tsp freshly ground black pepper

Directions

In a medium bowl, whisk together all ingredients except mayonnaise. Add mayonnaise and adjust seasoning to taste.

Italian Vinaigrette Salad Dressing

1 cup Extra Virgin Olive Oil
¼ cup raw apple cider vinegar (use more or less to taste)
2 tbsp roasted garlic OR 1-2 Cloves fresh garlic, minced
½ tsp salt
¼ tsp black pepper
1 tsp dried basil
1 tsp dried thyme
1 tsp dried rosemary
1 tsp dried oregano
2 tbsp fresh lemon juice
2 tbsp applesauce or coconut nectar

Directions

Mashup garlic with a fork and add coconut nectar or applesauce. Add spices and mash to combine. Add in rest of ingredients and mix well. Store in refrigerator and use as needed.

****DO NOT use fresh herbs it will taste completely different.

Ranch Dressing

½ cup cashews, soaked for 2-3 hours and drained
⅓ cup water
¼ cup almond milk (or other non-dairy milk)
1-2 cloves garlic
1 tbsp fresh parsley
1 tbsp fresh chives
1 tsp dried dill
½ lemon, juiced
½ tsp raw apple cider vinegar
½ tsp sea salt
Directions
Fresh ground pepper to taste With the exception of parsley, chives and dill, add all other ingredients in a high-speed blender. Blend until smooth. If you like thinner dressing, add a little water at a time until desired consistency is reached. Add herbs and pulse. Season with salt & pepper. Adjust according to taste. Chill for an hour. Use within 2 days. Store in fridge in an air-tight container.

Lemon-Garlic Dressing

½ cup olive oil
1 lemon, juiced
3 cloves garlic, chopped
Salt/pepper, to taste
Directions
In a food processor or chopper, combine all ingredients and blend until there are no garlic pieces left. Store in fridge.

Basil Salad Dressing

2 oz fresh basil
¾ cup olive oil
½ tsp sea salt
½ tsp pepper
1 tsp lemon juice
Blend on high speed until smooth.

Creamy Avocado Dressing

1 avocado
3 tbsp olive oil
1 tbsp lemon juice
¼ tsp black pepper Sea salt, to taste
½ c water
Directions
Place avocado, olive oil, lemon juice and water in a blender. Puree until smooth. Then blend in salt and pepper.

Creamy Onion Dressing

2 tbsp red onion
¼ cup apple cider vinegar
1 tbsp coconut aminos
1 tsp mustard powder
½ tsp sea salt
½ cup olive oil
Directions
Place onion, vinegar, coconut nectar, mustard and salt in blender and puree on high speed until smooth. While blending, drizzle in olive oil.

Italian Dressing

¼ cup apple cider vinegar
2/3 cup extra virgin olive oil
2 tbsp water
2 tbsp coconut aminos
2 tbsp of Italian seasoning
Combine all ingredients in salad shaker bottle, shake & enjoy.

Roasted Garlic Marinade

1 fist roasted garlic, mashed up in oil used to roast
3 sprigs or 2 tsp rosemary, chopped
3 sprigs or 1 ½ tsp sage, chopped
1 tsp Thyme
¼ tsp paprika
1 tsp salt
⅛ tsp black pepper
1 tbsp lemon juice
1 tbsp extra virgin olive oil
Rub marinade on meat at least 1 hour or up to 24 hours before roasting meat.

Stir Fry Sauce

2 cup chicken broth
2 cloves garlic
1 tsp grated ginger
1 tsp crushed red pepper
¼ cup coconut sugar
½ cup coconut aminos
3 tbsp Arrowroot powder (aka arrowroot starch)
3 tbsp warm water
Directions
Add all liquid ingredients to pot except the arrowroot starch and water. Wait to mix those up. Bring ingredients to a soft boil. Mix together arrowroot starch and warm water in a small dish and mix until starch is dissolved. Add arrowroot starch mixture to sauce mixture on stove and stir as it thickens.
Reduce heat to simmer and simmer until reduced to desired thickness. (Note: Sauce will thicken considerably as it cools)
Add to your favorite stir fry dish and enjoy!

You can start out with nothing and with no way, a way will be made.
   -Michael Beckwith

One of my favorite quotes! It's about having the cojones to show up as the brightest, happiest version of yourself and do whatever it takes to make your goals/dreams come true.
   I hope you enjoy this book for years to come

                                    Jessie
                                      xo

Kitchen Hacks!!!!

Basic Conversions
1 tbsp = 3 tsp
4 tbsp = ¼ cup
1 cup = 8 oz
2 cups = 1 pint
4 quarts = 1 gallon

1 Quart Conversions =
2 pints
4 cups
32 ounces
.95 liters

1 Pint Conversions =
2 cups
16 ounces
480 ml

1 Cup Conversions =
16 tbsp
½ pint
8 ounces
240 ml

Butter to Olive Oil Conversion Chart

Butter
1 tsp
1 tbsp=1/8 stick
2 tbsp=¼ stick
¼ cup=½ stick
½ cup=1 stick
⅔ cup= 1 ¾ sticks
¾ cup- 1 ½ sticks
1 cup= 2 sticks

Oil
¾ tsp
2 ½ tsp
1 ½ tbsp
3 tbsp
¼ cup + 2 tbsp
½ cup
½ cup = 1 tbsp
¾ cup

How to Half A Recipe
¼ cup = 2 tbsp
⅓ cup = 2 tbsp and 2 tsp
½ cup = ¼ cup
⅔ cup = ⅓ cup
¾ cup = 6 tbsp
1 tsp =½ tsp
½ tsp = ¼ tsp

Healthy Substitutes and yet still delicious!

1 Egg = 1 Banana
1 Cup Butter = 1 Cup Applesauce
1 Cup Butter = 1 Cup Avocado
1 Cup Butter = 1 Cup Greek Yogurt.

Trick to cutting Bakery bread

Turn the loaf upside down and cut it on the soft side. This saves the bread from getting squished and makes it much easier to cut.

Crockpot Time Conversion Chart

Oven	Low	High
15 - 30 min	4-6 hours	1-2 hours
30 - 60 min	5-7 hours	2-3 hours
1-2 hours	6-8 hours	3-4 hours
2-3 hours	8-10 hours	4-5 hours
4 hours	12 hours	6 hours

Over Salt your soup?

Throw a few potato slices in. The starch will soak up the extra salt, then just remove them before you eat.

A space for your favorite recipes & notes!

A space for your favorite recipes & notes!

A space for your favorite recipes & notes!

A space for your favorite recipes & notes!

A space for your favorite recipes & notes!

A space for your favorite recipes & notes!

A space for your favorite recipes & notes!

A space for your favorite recipes & notes!

She Hustles pg89